AF613993

Other books by Dave Morrison:
SWEET
Brand New Day
Sliver
the Lonely Life of Spies
Black Boat Black Water Black Sand
SIX
Clubland (first and second editions)

fail

poems by
Dave Morrison

JukeBooks

2012 JukeBooks
 Published in the United States by JukeBooks and lulu Press.

Grateful acknowledgements are due to the editors of the following publications where some of these poems first appeared:

Pride and Passion Anthology (Someday Soon)
Uni-Verse (Keith Moon, Untitled & Unfinished)
Hospital Drive Literary Journal (Writer Puts His Back Out)

Library of
Congress Cataloging-in-Publication Data

Morrison, Dave

fail / Dave Morrison

ISBN 978-1-105-84497-3

For more information about Dave Morrison please visit
www.dave--morrison.com
www.jukebookspublishing.weebly.com

As always, for Susan.

With special thanks to Alice Persons and Ted Bookey

"Hell, there are no rules here - we're trying to accomplish something."
Thomas A. Edison

Contents

52 Years Old

Last night I found a story I
had written a few years ago
about a teenage boy trying
to be a man, and not succeeding
exactly but making a manly
attempt, and it made me feel
a bit sad and lost (like the
character, actually) and I
wondered if I will ever be
wise or peaceful?

Then it occurred to me that
maybe I'm better off as I
am. I ache. I stumble. I
laugh. I move to loud music.
I'm a smart-ass. I'm 52
years old.

Bukowski wrote almost every
day, and let's face it, a lot of
it is not great poetry, but it
sure as hell is Bukowski through
and through. And maybe that's
the best we can ask for, to be
constantly ourselves. Rather than
ask "Is this good, or good enough,
or as good as so-and-so?" maybe
the only real question is "Is it
me? Is it truly me?", and if the
answer is Yes, or even better,
Hell Yes, then important
work has been done.

Because we cannot always be
wise or beautiful or clever,
but we can be ourselves. Our job
is to write those poems that only
we can write; otherwise they won't
be written, and the vast human

story will not be as complete as
it will be if we keep the pen
wiggling across the small
white dance floor of the page.

Advice

You think you're in
like Flynn? Got it
made in the shade?
Wise up.
Get real.
Snap out of it.
You think you're in
the catbird seat? You're
living the life of
Riley?
Get a grip.
Simmer down.
Watch your step.
You think you're on
easy street? In the
pink?
Smarten up.
Mind your Ps and Qs.
Look sharp.

Get with it.
Watch your mouth.
Now, beat it.

Autumn

The wind hisses through
the trees like a great dark
snake coiling around the
house, patient and
cool.

The green leaves of summer
are rattling brown husks, ghosts
crouch on roof ridges and
gnaw acorns, the dim glow
of the streetlights looks like the
lights of a sinking ship.

"Let go," the night
whispers, "crawl in a
hole and go to sleep…"
but for me the restless
wind that smells of cold
earth and rotting apples is
like strong black coffee
that makes me want to
stay up late so the moon
can watch me through the
window.

These are the nights that we
turn up our collars, these
are the nights when we
haunt our own dreams,
these are the nights when
possibilities hang under
the eaves like bats.

Backstage

Had he been seated in
the balcony he would have seen
a goddess in the halo of
the spotlight, part flesh,
part hologram; iridescent
white gown, graceful arms
golden hair floating about
her face like light, her voice
as clear and true as a bell.

Had the audience been
standing where he was in the
wings they would have seen
the blemishes, the bulges, the
artful makeup a mask of
youth.

No matter - backstage he
had seen her sitting on the
stairs assuring her little one
that she would be home in two
days and when she was she would
hold him *so tight*, smiling into the
phone while a single tear drew
a line through the makeup,
and the stagehand crept
away but what he wanted to do was
applaud.

Benefit Show Saturday Night

She stood on the side of the
stage like a shy heron;
long-limbed and almost
weightless, somewhere between
elegant and awkward,
tapping her foot and doing
nervous things with
her hands.

You wondered if she was
one of the players' girlfriend
until she picked her way through
the cables to the microphone
and opened her mouth and
out came honey and brass,
the loveliest version of
Angel From Montgomery
you've ever heard.

She wore that song like a gauzy dress.
She blushed at the applause.

Book

I'm throwing away a book
of poetry. It's old and worn, I
don't think the library would
take it for their book sale.
Old flags are destroyed with
respectful ceremony at
the American Legion - should there be
an organization of old writers and
English teachers who lovingly burn
broken books while standing at
attention?
But what if it's not a good
book, what if it was read so
many times because some English
teacher who really wanted to be
a screenwriter just kept
assigning it because the ancient
department head did?
Well-loved books get taped
together again and again, and
finally read in pieces.
This one?
Thirty or so years ago some
chemist came up with a new
way to put out fires in libraries;
instead of spraying water everywhere
and damaging books, the suppression
system would spray a gas that
sucked the oxygen out of the room,
denying the fire what it needed to
live, thereby snuffing out the flame.
Problem;
If there was a custodian pushing a
broom through the stacks, he too
would be denied what he needed
to live, and his flame would be
snuffed out.
I'm that custodian, and in this
book are poems that emit that
gas, poems that suck the

air out of a room.
I have to throw it away before
some innocent reader finds
it and decides that this
is what poetry is supposed
to be.

Born For It

I needed to find out
who I was and what
I was supposed to do -
not knowing any better
I set out to try to do
everything I was
asked.

As a boy I learned
that I was not meant
to be a simple or
pleasing son.

I learned that I was
not meant to excel
in school. I learned
that I was not good
with money or
business, that I was
not meant to finish
long or difficult
projects.

I was not meant to
be carefree, or
graceful.

As a young man I
learned that I was
not designed to be
a selfless, generous
or honest lover. I
was not meant to
work a job that
paid well.

I was not sure of much,
I was not thick-skinned,
I was not peaceful or

brave.

I don't mean to say that
I didn't learn anything -
far from it.
I had gifts.

I was sometimes
charming, I was a likable
smart-ass, I had the
beginnings of a
decent criminal
imagination.

I was a pretty good
dreamer and drinker.
I had an extensive
jukebox in my head,
I could make music and
tell stories. I had
moments of love and
clarity and energy.
Even joy.

If this were some sort
of aptitude survey it
would have a happy
ending. I was born
to be humble and
heartbroken and grateful.
I was born to spend
half my time in a
hidden mystical world.

I was meant to build
kites from words and
raise them into the
wind.

Whatever this is,
I was born for it.

Climbing

(for Alex Honnold)

Force a finger into a fissure
one digit deep, not even,
the amount of finger pad it
takes to ring a doorbell
now steadies you against a
hard wall that looks and feels
like a massive tombstone, suspends
you above a vision straight out
of a dream, world with no bottom,
senses singing like a taut wire, there
is nothing but this crack, this
thumb-sized stub, the soft tug of the
chalk bag, there is no triumphant
conclusion, no hauling yourself
to the miraculous top, there is
no whistling wind and broken
doll death, there is only the
next step, the next finger-hold,
the next two feet, the sun
sparkling on the specks of
quartz.
Breathe.
Concentrate.

Coast

Water dimpled pewter
sky gray felt
wind stiff bristle brush
the cold embraces you
like a strange but not
unwelcome friend,
the harbor empty, even
of birds - this is not a day
one sees in the tourist
brochures or calendar
pages, but it is beautiful,
not for what it offers,
but maybe for what
it asks.

Dangerous Friend

He's going to blow, I've
got a bad feeling, and I
don't know what can be
done - he's been hollowed out
by the carpenter ants of
anger and addiction and
parasites and ghosts have
moved in.
He wears sunglasses for the
same reason poker players
do - to give nothing away,
to give no advance warning,
as if surprise is the only
weapon he has left - yet
he's telegraphing something
odd, uploading video after
video; Don't Worry Be Happy,
On Top Of The World, Happy
Shiny People, etc.
Days ago he told everyone who
didn't visit him in jail to go
fuck themselves, even those
of us (most of us?) who had
no idea.
A snarling snapping dog
wagging its tail.
Not always - once kind and
quiet and helpful. So now we feel
the vertigo that he feels. He has
worn us out as he must feel worn
out. To back off is to play a
non-speaking role in his self-fulfilling
noir novel. To take part is to feel
suckered. There's no way to avoid
shuffling through the Fuck You
dance, there's no right move.

Including doing nothing.
Including doing something.

Including trying to know.
He is pissing in the well and
probably can't help it.

Epiphany

I struggled with it,
it was my own fault for
rushing, something went
wrong and suddenly I was
somersaulting down the
spiral staircase of failure,
doing what I always do;
getting angry, getting
heartbroken, furious and
ashamed and making it
worse.
Then, something beautiful
happened - I gave up.
I quit. I had fucked it up
and that was that. I made
tea and sat down with a
book and felt better.
I practiced what I would say
when my wife got home and
asked "How'd it go?"
Disaster, I will say, it's
ruined, the whole thing
has to be done over, it's
an ugly mess, a waste
of time.
I can't wait to hear her
key in the lock. And next time
I will embrace failure sooner,
instead of treating it like an
obnoxious drunken friend
you have to make
excuses for.

Fail

I failed once.
I failed twice.
I failed three times, and
each time it was something
dear to me that felt like a
vital organ that I
couldn't live without.
I carried each failure like
a loved one I had crippled.

These were not things that
were taken away from me, I
did not suffer bad luck or
misfortune.
I failed.
I gave up.
I bailed, I chickened out, I lost my
nerve, my will, my vision.
I wasn't strong enough.
I did not endure.
I failed.

These may be my greatest gifts;
the forest is burned to ash, the
dilapidated house is demolished,
the slate is wiped clean.
I can begin. I am newborn, a
virgin, a rookie, a beginner;
I am promising.

I have chucked all the broken
furniture and ill-fitting clothes
overboard, and my bright balloon
rises into the morning sky. Now
I am light, and that makes me
fast and strong. I have closed an old
account, thrown away dried tubes
of paint, I have taken the unwieldy
contraption to the dump, I have

cleared my workbench.

I can look back fondly; Man,
I really screwed the pooch, that
one went up in flames, missed the
mark, didn't work for beans.

It failed.
I failed.
And I am grateful - I can
make way for the next few
failures that will undoubtedly
lead to some surprising,
sweeter success.

Fly

My father was an ordinary man.
Good, sweet even, but not particularly
smart or ambitious.

My mother was beautiful and unhappy.
Maybe she had guessed wrong
about him.

I don't suppose she thought about getting pregnant.
I don't think she foresaw the
ordinary man, the ordinary apartment.

Every day she heard a 'whoosh' sound.
That was time and opportunity
passing her by.

In one way my father was not ordinary.
He could fly.
I was the only one who knew.

One night when they fought I couldn't sleep.
In the wee hours I heard someone
pad through the apartment.

I followed my father.
Up the stairs to the roof where
he stood on the parapet.

I tried to yell but couldn't.
He was finally going to escape
the put-downs and disdain.

He took a deep breath.
All I could think was, "this
is the beginning of death in my life".

Then I saw him land on the roof across the street.
He was as graceful as a diver or trapeze
artist, but without the pool or wires.

I saw him do it five or six times that year.
It seemed exhilarating and
soothing at the same time.

He didn't drink or fight or fool around.
This was the way he got free of the
daytime world that gave him so little.

Maybe the beauty and love was gone from his marriage.
He could love the air that rushed past him,
the freedom, the speed.

One morning they found his body.
I couldn't tell them that it was no
suicide.

He'd simply forgotten
his glasses.

For the 9 Year-Old Victim

We are capable of
decency, kindness, bravery
and love, great love.
There is good in the world,
and it always, eventually
wins.
This is what I tell myself when
I need comfort, when some of
us act like rabid dogs, when I
recognize the same fear and
violence that killed you
crouching in my confused
heart.

I Could Have Danced All Night

It happens now and then,
I'll get a song stuck in my
head that is totally out of
the blue - not on my ipod,
I didn't hear it on the radio
or in the grocery store, it's
just there, like a mysterious
package left on your doorstep,
or a stray dog that follows you
home and sits in your driveway.
In this case it's an old Broadway
show tune, and all I can think is
that Pop has come back to visit
me in the only way he knows -
shared music. When I was small
he would play reel-to-reel tapes
to send me off to sleep: South
Pacific, Oklahoma, Music Man,
My Fair Lady.
Pop was an unapologetic cornball
who loved these velveteen tunes -
he'd sing his favorite two or three
lines over and over, and now I'm
thinking about spreading my wings
and doing a thousand things that
I've never even considered. I'd
wash these songs right out of
what's left of my hair, but I
don't want to, because just like
when I was five and my eyes
closed bringing darkness to
an already dark room while
the reels went around and around
I can't see Pop, but I know that
he's listening too.

Idleness or Art?

So you find a bit of
stick and you sit on
an overturned bucket
outside your back door,
you open your pocketknife
and begin to whittle, turning
the stick over in your hands
and watching the wood chips
fall on your shoes.
Before long the bit of stick
suggests to you that
hidden in the curves is
a leaping fish, and sure enough,
you carve away the wood that
covers it and
there it is.
So it's like that - sometimes
you don't so much set out
to do a thing; you just decide
to take part in a process
and see where it
leads you.

Job

She worked in a convenience
store on the moon.
She was the only one who
answered the ad.
She dusted shelves and
washed out the coffee
pots, put the posters in
the windows that advertised
seasonal specials.
She threw out a lot of fruit.
She stopped stocking dairy.
She was literally bored to
tears, but the paychecks
came like clockwork.

Judas Outside the Garden

Those loving bumblers, those
well-intentioned students don't
understand that if Master lives to
a ripe old age it will all be for
nothing - the opportunity to tip
the world on this holy fulcrum will
be lost, and it has to happen
tonight.

Who among them has the guts to
damn themselves, shame themselves
for eternity so scores of less deserving
can have hope?

He will suffer horribly but briefly
on the cross and I will hang from that
scrawny tree for all time. Mine is the
deepest and most bitter love of all, and
this is our secret.

Who is more alone? If only
I could give the vultures
names.

Keith Moon

Imagine swallowing lightning
and having to carry it around
all day, waiting for the

moment you can
turn it loose. A wild cross
between a juvenile

delinquent and a Hindu
god with a drumstick in
each hand, his technique

was not a choice or plan
but simply what happened
when the mad genie was

let out of the bottle.
If Keith Moon could have
played drums all day,

every day he'd still be
here; a short-circuited
Energizer Bunny behind the

kit, sweating it out and
finding some semblance of
a deafening peace.

Which raises the question:
how many hyperactive trouble-
makers could be geniuses if given

the right tools?

Longing

The dog lifts her head.
She hears something that
we can't; it is faint, or
far away, disappearing into
the distance perhaps, but
the dog hears it.

The dog is no fool - she knows
that there is no way to
find it, catch it, run it down,
but that doesn't stop her
from wanting that more
than anything.

The dog puts her head down
on her paws. In that instant
the house grows smaller and
her heart swells. She will
chase it tonight in
her dreams.

Marathon Man

God, I loved to run.
Ever since I was young.
I was built to do it.
It took me away from my
worries and fears, real or
imagined, and left me too
winded to care about
small problems.
Running didn't just
take me away from troubling
situations or people; it felt
great - the dizzying speed,
the sweet blur, the rush.
I ran and ran and it barely
showed - I made it look
easy. I discovered that I
knew lots of people who
loved to run, some as much
as I did. It got to the point
where I'd rather run than
eat, rather run than sleep,
rather run than just about
anything.
It kept me young and loose,
or so I thought.
At some point I realized that
while my desire to run wasn't
aging, my body was. There were
fewer people to run with. I
didn't bounce back as fast as
I once had. Too much of a
good thing.
So running isn't a part of
my life much any more,
even though I still
love it. Things change.
Maybe I changed.

Sorry, did I say running?
I meant drinking.

My Jump Rope Song

last of four - suburban town
skinny eager classroom clown
underachiever sharp as a pin
these days I'd have Ritalin

cigarettes, liquor, vandalism
bookworm werewolf teenage schism
menial jobs at minimum wage
saved by putting words on a page

No Vacancy

Cars slow down to look
confused by the empty lot
and the No Vacancy sign

I sit behind drawn curtains
watch potential customers
drive off in disappointment

It's no way to run a business
but I just can't bear to look
after your needs right now.

Poetry Let Me Down

He asked me why
I drink.

It's a tarp, I say, tied
over a pile of feathers
in the wind.

Turns out no
cop wants to
hear that.

Poetry Rocks

The poet from the mainland
sat in the cab of the ancient
pickup bumping along the

remote island's one road, holding
the typewritten invitation.
"This is a big honor for me...

usually I read for a handful of
people in the library. I think it's
amazing that your whole town

comes out for a poetry reading.
How often do you do this?"
"Once a year!" the geezer behind

the wheel wheezed happlly.
In a meadow at one end of
the island chairs and a platform

had been set up, and a crowd
was waiting.
After each poem the crowd

cheered enthusiastically - the
poet could feel the excitement
building. He thought "This is

amazing - they love poetry. They
love *my* poetry!"
When he finished they rushed

the stage and lifted him onto
their shoulders chanting
"Poetry Rocks! Poetry Rocks!"

Drunk with happiness he
chanted along with them,

pumping his fist in the air.

They carried him to a cliff
overlooking a striking and
rugged stone formation

hundreds of feet below,
known to the locals as
Poetry Rocks.

Months later, the ancient
postmistress sat at her
typewriter.

"Dear Madam, we have all
read your latest collection,"
she picked up the slim volume, made

a face, and threw it into the woodstove,
"and we'd like to invite you to our
annual Poetry celebration."

Prediction

Things will get better
things will get worse
things will be fine
countries will crumble
babies will be born
lies will be told
heroic deeds will be done
hearts will be broken
new things will be invented
old truths will be rediscovered
swindlers will prosper
frauds will be exposed
masterpieces will be created
leaves will fall
wars will start
wars will end
the rich will get richer
we will elect the wrong people
there will be new sources of hope
some people will die too soon
some people will live too long
love will endure
the planet will suffer
brand new green things will push up through the dirt
everything will end, and begin again.
In short, more of the same.

Present

Some people, who
are smarter and more
peaceful than I, say
that the best and healthiest
place to be is in
the Present Moment. The
Here and Now.

I get it, I do;
reliving the past and
fretting about the future
are like writing a novel
on an ice cube - it's just
not a good use of time,
especially in the summer.

I want to be in the
Here and Now (and
it's not just because I'm
paying rent), I want to
be sensible and healthy
but here's the thing;
the times I feel like the
real me, the times I feel
most connected to the
cosmos, with my finger
in the creative socket, the
times I feel closest to God
are those times when I
have one foot in the Here
and Now and the other in
some dimension that I
cannot name, some odd and
timeless place not of this
world, or possibly parallel
and invisible, glimpsed
through a knothole or
through the crack under a

drawn shade, a reflection
in a mirror in the corner
of my eye, and it is not
home, but it is not
unwelcoming either, a
place I have inhabited in
some other time and
place, just not Here,
or Now.

To live wholly in this
mirror-place would be
madness for sure, but
for me to live only in
this place is a sort of
madness also.

So, I will do my best to
live in the present, to be
aware and attentive and
grateful; joyful, playful,
reverent...

I will, however, have to
revisit my definitions of
Here
and
Now.

Pursuit

So many poems are like
birds that fly in one
open window and out

another, glimpsed but
not grasped. If I catch
any at all it is usually the

slow, the dull, the lame,
and that is what keeps
me writing; the possibility

of capturing the
brilliant, the beautiful,
the swift.

Quote Me

Writing poetry without
form is like having
a boxing match
without a ring.
Of course it's not
really a ring, and
it's not really
necessary to
the action.

Rabbit

Nature is just as
cold and practical
as her wayward son,
Man.

The strong kill the
weak, the fast kill the
slow, the young maul
the old.

This seems somehow more
noble (a romantic human notion),
more practical in
Nature.

The coyote kills the rabbit
because he is hungry, not
because of the rabbit's religion
or sex or politics.

Does it matter to the rabbit?
Or just to us, the
supermarket shoppers?

Regret

If I could go back in
time and change just
one thing that I've done,
I would go back to when I
was six years old, and I
stole some money from
my grandmother's change
cup so I could go to this
gas station down the street
where they sold candy -
my grandfather found me
squatting in front of the
candy rack at Lester's and
angrily asked me what
would make me run away
like that and he hauled me
out into the sunshine.
What I should have done
was to grab his hand and
leap into the air pulling
him behind me, and we would
have flown over his house,
and the Ray-O-Vac factory
and the new shopping
center, so high that we would
see Lake Champlain in one
direction and Canada in the
other, then I would have
set him down gently in his
yard so that when we went in
and my grandmother asked us
what we'd been doing, he'd
have to mumble
"nothing."

Restless

The car keys burn
in your hand like a
murder weapon, your
brain says "don't you
dare, put them down" but
the pit of your stomach
says "LET'S GO"; these
rooms are plastered with
defeat and out there is a
night that beckons like a
beautiful woman wearing
just a hint of perfume - OK
forget that, it's not that, it's
possibility, it's air that hasn't
already been breathed, it's
something more, something
different, something better,
something or someone or
somewhere that doesn't
belong to anyone yet but
could belong to you, and
right now you own nothing
of value, you have an
inheritance that you don't
want, you're wearing someone
else's clothes and reciting
someone else's lines, you're
trying to be a good sport but
the water is rising above your
belt, you see what I mean?
This isn't about fun, or adventure,
this is about survival - if you don't
think it's about saving your life,
then at least consider that it's
about saving your identity, your
chances, saving your ass.
Just go.
Go *now*.

Rex Goliath

Here's the thing;
It's enough work for me to
feel something, let alone
think about the feeling, then
describe the thoughts about
the feeling, then transform the
words that describe the thoughts
about the feeling into some kind
of structure, some kind of
vehicle that can transport
another person, make them
somehow share the thoughts
about the feeling, maybe even the
feeling itself.
See? I'm tired already. I'm tired just
trying to deal with the feelings,
plural, because it's not just one,
good God no, it's one right after
another, like cars on a highway
that you're trying to limp across.
Is it any wonder? I need to work and
sleep and talk to my wife and take
care of the house, when the hell am
I supposed to find the time to think
about feelings, then describe them, then
craft a good poem?
Are you kidding me? Then I'm supposed
to get them out into the world in some
orderly fashion?

Here's what I have to say to that:
In our grocery store is a nice
merlot called Rex Goliath -
it's $8.99 a bottle, which isn't
bad. Sometimes it even
goes on sale.

She Was Right

In her heart
she believed
two things:

that she deserved
her heart's desire
and that she would
not have it.

She lived in a
constant cycle of
dismissed opportunity
and hurt.

Sadly, she showed
that she was right,
and she was right.

Someday Soon

I finally met someone
and for whatever reason,
or for a hundred reasons,

I believed that this was the
person I could give myself to,
be better with; a partner to

love and be loved by, a
co-navigator, someone
to grow old with.

But as much as we were
encouraged and ready to
accept one another, we were

not encouraged or accepted.
The clergyman thought he was
being helpful by suggesting

some alternative, as he did not
approve of our union. In a
world desperate for love he

needed tradition to trump
respect, devotion, tenderness,
loyalty, dreams.

All I can say is this; his commitment
to the church lasted another
year - ours twenty-four so far.

The audacity of our love? One
of us brought up Catholic, one
Methodist, but it could have

been any unimportant detail
that makes another
uncomfortable.

Someday soon I hope that
we learn to pay attention
to the right things.

Sparkle

In my rearview the
glass company truck creeps
up on my ass, the driver
playing air-drums to some
rock song with lots of cymbal
crashes, and I begin to imagine
the driver getting so into the
drum solo that he stomps the
brake imagining it to be a
kick drum pedal, which sends
the truck into a figure skater
spin that is stopped by a
telephone pole.
The driver is wearing a seatbelt,
good man, so he's fine, I don't
want any harm to come to him,
I just want to see all that glass
shattered, barrels of sparkling
gems, everything as glittery as
a showgirl's dress, dusted with
powdered chandelier, like a
galaxy spilled on the
road.

Strange Day

When I got home from
work my house looked
different - it was surrounded

by droopy old trees, and all
the doors were crooked.
When I stepped

inside I heard music from
the kitchen, and when I went
there my grandfather rushed

me - he was naked and had
a big knife. He chased me
through the house until I

found myself out on the
front lawn and the house
looked normal again.

That night I had a
dream that I made a
sandwich, read the paper
and went to bed.

Submission

The poem came to me with
its little suitcase packed.
I knew what this meant -
it had happened before.
It wanted to go out into the world
and seek its fortune.

There were stories the
poems told each other about
magazines and radio and
being memorized by students.
The unfinished poems who
would never go out into the
world told the other stories, but
no one listened to them.

They told stories of poems that
simply disappeared, poems that
were rejected, mocked, dissected.
"Sour grapes" the new poems said,
"not true."

I addressed the envelope and
the poem climbed in.
"Good luck" I sighed. The poem
held up its little thumb like
a brave astronaut.

It breaks your heart sometimes.

The Moment

I don't envy those
people who are certain
of what will happen
to them when they
die, who know exactly
what to expect.

All I can guess is
this; one day the machine
will break, or stop, there
will be a punch in the
chest, or a bad pain or
a distracted driver or a
little piece of me will
break loose in my
bloodstream, or who
knows - maybe I'll be lucky
and just go to sleep.

And when that happens,
when the curtain is
drawn, when the electricity
clicks off, what then?
Will it be like walking out
into the stands at Fenway
on a beautiful summer day,
or like diving into warm black
ink, will it be like Star Wars
hyperspace, or a disco dance floor
or twirling Maria in the Sound of
Music? Or absolute Nothing?
No sound no light no heat
no thing?

It beats the hell out of me, and
that , my friends, is the gift
of Mystery, because by not
knowing, the moment of
my death will be my
greatest adventure.

The Old Artist

The old artist finally
admitted that his fame
and wealth just left him
feeling like he'd eaten
too much too quickly.

"It was a bit of a joke,"
he said, "I made money and
I got laid and to a young
man that is everything. The
wealthy and unoccupied
wanted whatever was exotic
strange and new, so I gave it
to them."

"It doesn't give me pleasure
now. I could have done
better, my work could have
meant more than simply
being provocative. I found
a hundred new ways of
saying 'fuck you', and most
of them are hanging in museums."

"No one dared admit that what
they saw was exactly what it
looked like - if there was no
meaning they invented one.
That's where the real work
was, the creativity; imagining
purpose in the jumble..."

Years later Jimi Hendrix said
essentially the same thing: he
would play guitar behind his head,
with his teeth, all the razzmatazz and
bullshit, and if the audience ate
it up he'd give up on them - the
fuckers only wanted a *show*.

But if the tricks were met with
silence he would abandon them
and transcendently play
his ass off.

It's up to the audience: if
we continue to pay for crap
then crap is what we'll get.
If we applaud hokum and hubris,
we will drown in it. But if we
save our love for the
real thing, we just might
get it.

The Old Depression

This isn't so bad.

I feel a bit blue-
I used to feel black, like
the inside of a furnace, or
the bottom of a mineshaft,
like a vacuum in space, I
used to feel like
Satan had turned himself into
a gang of carpenter ants who
were eating through my bone
marrow on their way to
my gasping heart.

This isn't so bad - I have
a pain like a pulsing blue light
under my breastbone - the
Old Depression used to
rattle my teeth, singe my
eyebrows, force me to swallow
fish hooks and slam my
fingers in a door.
Yeah, I'm feeling sad and weary,
but I used to feel broken and foul,
like a crushed skunk dying by
the side of the road.

The Old Depression pounded
nails into the back of my skull.
The Old Depression suggested all
manner of ways I could stop being such
a burden to the living. The Old
Depression loved me so much it
didn't want to let me go, even as
it leapt from the high ledge.

This isn't so bad.
I'll be fine.

Time Keeper

I keep a watch in a
drawer, waiting, I
suppose, for my shiny
new one to fail so it can
come out and guide me
once more through my
day, reminding me of
the insistent forward
march of life, helping
me to connect by
being in the right
place at the
right time.
Until then the watch
lies in the black-sock
darkness with no sound
except its own tiny
metallic heartbeat,
counting, counting,
counting.
I've got to get him
out of there.
I don't know what's
worse - blind and alone
in the drawer, or one of
a hundred in a box or
display case, all making
that little announcement
every second - *still here,*
still here... like a
drunken audience that
can't clap in sync.

Truth In Advertising

I pledge allegiance
to the flag, which
on closer inspection
resembles a large $100 bill
and to the Republic
which started out as
such a wonderful idea,
one nation, now trapped
under the followers of
one god, easily divisible
with liberty and justice
for all wealthy white
straight Christian
men.

Untitled and Unfinished

The rope swing wasn't
intended to be used in
the winter, but that doesn't

matter now, as the wind
whistles past his ears and
the hemp bites into his fingers.

At one end of the arc is a
hole cut in the ice, and at
the other , a bonfire:

he is wearing himself out
avoiding one, then
the other.

At this point I'm going to
have to ask you to finish the
poem by constructing a

pithy clever moral to help
the next fool. On the bright side
it doesn't have to rhyme.

Unused poem notes

First,
I say goodbye to
friends and neighbors -
I do this by giving them the
usual wave, but it is loaded with
an inaudible message, much in
the same way that you might
hide a dog's pill in a ball of
hamburg; the goodbye is
there but it won't register until
some other change is noticed
and connected.
"Goodbye for now" goes the
message, "I need some quiet and
some rest and out here it's all
wasps and typewriters and
out-of-tune violins - I have
to screw shut the hatches on
my little submarine and descend
into the cool darkness."

Bye!

* * *

Then
I decide that nothing
matters except the quiet,
which is really just an idea,
as it is never totally quiet.
The sound, the static, the
chatter is like water in a
reservoir - if you can drain it,
lower it, you will find the
little town that was in the
valley before they built the
dam; bell swinging slowly,
limp wet flag on the monument
pole, everything intact and whole,
no longer hidden

* * *

I pass through memories
like one passes through strange
towns, one after another,
hoping to find the star
on the map.
So grateful.
So bitter.
So lost.
So expectant.

* * *

The fatigue saves me.
The weariness at all the
bullshit protects me.
If I had more energy
what would I do - fight it?
You might as well
fistfight the rain.
When I was young I
would drink and stay up and
smoke out the open window
and ask why? Why? Why?
Now I go
to sleep.

Good night.

Waiting

I'm waiting.
Now I'm writing.
I'm writing about waiting.

I'm waiting for a poem,
or several, waiting for words
like magic bricks that
arrange themselves into
a building, or a block
of marble that sheds
everything but the
form within.

I'm realistic - I don't think
much will come of it - but
as a writer I must write even
if it's more like vandalizing
a perfectly good
blank page.

My pen is like a narrow
sewer pipe, and I know
that someone has dropped
a diamond ring in a toilet;
I have to wait and watch
and believe.
And catch it.

Weariness

My bones feel
hollow and are
ringing with bad
electricity, humming with
fatigue.

I have to
reassess. There were
things I wanted
to do but
one has to
be realistic. You
can't throw a
piano. You can't
run up a
wall.

I'm losing the
battle with gravity.
My head is
too heavy for
my neck muscles
and my imagination
can only come
up with things like
chair
cigarette
TV
Sleep.

One's will shrivels
like a raisin.
Does it really
matter, this writing
of poems? No.
We are surrounded
by clusters of
words, and unless
they are spot-lit,
or full volume

do we notice
them, or does
it add to
the hum and
fizz and background
noise?

I'm too tired
to be angry
about how tired
I am. The
well is dry.
The ball has
rolled into a
corner and that's
where it will
stay.

It's all too
much work. The
vampire of the
work-week has
bled me dry.

Weather

I read my poems on Monday
and I was surprised and pleased
to discover that they were
well-constructed and fresh in
their approach, humorous but
with gravitas, clearly ready to
be published alongside the
darlings and heavy-hitters,
in fact, in a way that could
identify me as a darling and
a heavy-hitter.

I read them again on Wednesday
and wondered who had wiped
themselves with my notebook?
Sloppy, amateurish, these
so-called 'poems' aimed low
and missed. Do I really drink
that much that I imagined that
anyone would want to read them?

On Thursday it occurred to me
that the poems had not changed -
they were still whatever they were
when they first vibrated my antenna -
what had changed was my internal
weather, morphing from warm and
sunlit to drizzle and dank, a cloud
scuttling across the sun or a beam
piercing the fog, the change
of light, the tang in the air that
signals the death of a season or
a shift in conditions, a hint of chill
or sweat, the same things
that I discover and forget over and
over and over again.

Writer Puts His Back Out

From now on, all
he will be able to
write about is pain,
if he can even write
at all.

His wife asks, "Are
you all right? Do
you need any help?"
and all he can do is
grunt through gritted
teeth like a wounded
caveman.

The energy that used
to go towards constructing
good lines, or linking
observations, or even
daydreaming now goes
towards straining out of
the chair, or shuffling
to the bathroom.

He approaches each task as
if he is diffusing a bomb -
one wrong move, one
shift in balance and there
will be a blast of bright
yellow light.

He is astonished at
all the things he has
done in his life that
did not result in
lasting pain. He misses
his young body.

Soon he will fall
back on old habits.
He will think of his

vertebrae as rusted
ball bearings, his
sciatica as a jangling
toaster element, or a
telegraph of pain,
or some such thing.

For now he stares
out the window and
considers the complex
and wearying project
of making tea.

Writing Prompt

Go to your private room
the one that has been cleared
of all unnecessary things
the one with the window
that shows you the moon
the one with the old good furniture
and the small rug made by women
in Persia, reciting Hafiz
and the candles from the dime store
the books well-loved and chosen
the pens full of poems
and the paper waiting to receive them.

Go to your quiet room
the corners piled with whispers
the dim hiss of distant tires
kissing staying pavement
the spaces where the songs go
like empty trumpet cases
questions and suggestions
hung like coats on coat hooks.

Go to your holy room
where everything is possible
and everything is forgiven
and everything is acceptable
and nothing really matters
you can be as alone as the moon
and still part of a far-flung family
do something - do nothing
just do it with love and hunger.

About the Author

DM was born outside of Boston in 1959, and played in rock & roll bands in Boston and NYC. He now lives on the coast of Maine with his wife Susan. This is his eighth poetry collection. For more information please visit www.dave--morrison.com.

photo - Ken Gross

Clubland

Fighting Cock Press USA 2011

"Morrison's rock star past haunts much of his writing, but his eye for detail and his razor-sharp sense of humor elevate his words into something much more than that – something visceral and anchored in the real world, whether it's in the past or the present." (Emily Burnham – Bangor Daily News)

"Morrison can be trusted to not waste your time; every poem is worth the read. He never missteps in his wistful yet frank look at the bars, motels, managers, band members and girl friends that make up the world of Boston rock. It's a perfect book for late night with a drink..." (Paul Lovell -Boston Groupie News)

This collection will leave you feeling energized, buoyed up, sucked dry, exhausted, hungover and hopeful in turn, and finally, feeling that "all in all it's good to be alive/it's good to try, it's even good to fail." (Alice Persons, Editor and Publisher, Moon Pie Press)

So the poet must fight back...and that's precisely what Dave Morrison has done. By tapping into his tumultuous past, Morrison has created work that is not only technically sound, but viscerally engaging. His is no passive verse; it grabs you by the collar and demands your attention. It kicks in the door, puts its feet up on the table and turns the stereo up to 11. (Allen Adams MaineEdge)

http://clublandpoems.wordpress.com/

JukeBooks

Publishers of Fine Poetry Since 2006

www.jukebookspublishing.weebly.com

www.ingramcontent.com/pod-product-compliance
Ingram Content Group UK Ltd.
Pitfield, Milton Keynes, MK11 3LW, UK
UKHW040558210726
13854UKWH00008B/1390

9 781105 844973